WHAT IS DEFI?
GUIDES: HEX

JOAKIM KRISTIANSEN

YAK HAT

ACKNOWLEDGEMENTS

Christian and Rasmus. Micheal Lung, Taylor Kennedy, Jannika, Jorja, Edwin Haspels for excellent feedback.
And of course the Hexicans for filling in the gaps.

CONTENTS

ABOUT THE AUTHOR

Joakim Kristiansen is a teacher, book publisher and sustainable living warrior. A former gold bug/altcoin shiller/Bitcoin maximalist, he was introduced to the world of DeFi after listening to the 'Bankless' podcast. Since then, he has gone on to write What is DeFi? Guides to Bitcoin, Stablecoins and now his latest book on Hex.

An interest in monetary history and cryptocurrencies has led him to exciting places with interesting people. Whether that's with a group trying to reintroduce the gold Dinar into Pakistan, an anarchist conference in Mexico or installing Telegram.

Introduced to Bitcoin in 2014, he instantly moved his gold into crypto when he realised this will be the new money. Once in the crypto-sphere, he made all the common mistakes the uninitiated do when moving into the 'Wild West' of the 21st century, the world of altcoins. Mistakes the What is Defi? series hopes to help people avoid.

He has worked in the banking, construction,

energy, sales and education sectors, to name a few. He is currently publishing books on sustainable living and early years reading through his Yak Hat publishing company.

WHAT IS DEFI? GUIDES

Traders get 'Rekt'. How accurate is that statement? Well, according to the top 5 online trading platforms, it's on average 70% true. They proudly advertise the fact knowing that people don't care that much. People want those significant gains. They are sure that they are in the 30% of people who make gains while the rest lose all of their hard-earned savings.

Trading (as in the buying and selling of stocks and crypto for no other reason than price performance) adds very little value to society. Even when people make money trading, their wins come from one place, somebody else's losses. They may use that money to go on and give back to society or the businesses whose stock/coin price was the reason they earned in the first place, but not often.

All is not lost. There are still great ways to invest in crypto without depending on others' losses (or losses of the small investor). There are ways to grow your wealth without putting it "all on red" at the crypto roulette table. You can add liquidity to a liquidity pool, lend coins to a lending platform, or earn interest through staking, whether on a network or exchange. These are but a few of many examples that let the average person take advantage of the fastest-growing market globally in a safer manner.

What is DeFi? Guides inform the people who want to explore the world of cryptocurrency and decentralised finance in a sensible, measured way. But with thousands of projects out there, What is DeFi? Guides aim to hone in on some exciting projects with fundamental value propositions completed and currently being put to work. Not a promise of something on the way, but living, breathing cryptocurrencies fulfilling their intended (or perhaps otherwise) purpose right now.

What is DeFi? Guides are not investment suggestions, cryptocurrencies are volatile, and the events that affect their price cannot be guaranteed or even known. There is inherent risk when investing in them. But you can minimise that risk greatly by looking at projects that are already up and running and already have market fit. These guides will not promise any of the mentioned coins will go up in price. They are about tokens fulfilling one of the roles in the DeFi network and fulfilling them now.

The DeFi mentality is pretty simple. Banks and other financial institutions provide a whole host of services, from wealth storage, loans, facilitating trans-actions etc. DeFi aims to replace these services one by one with a crypto alternative (each service having its cryptocurrency).

Many could argue that Bitcoin will replace the currency, security and store of value (among other things), but what about other products banks offer like interest yielding savings accounts, pension investments or loans? DeFi can replace each of these services one by one. The DeFi 'movement', if you will, sets out to find more decentralised, efficient and fair financial products.

You may ask yourself, why do we need to replace the services of the bank? They seem to be doing a pretty good job and making sure one's money is secure and that we also get paid interest at the bank with little risk of losing our wealth.

Unfortunately, the money in your bank is subject to inflation, your savings account with $10,000 in it may now be worth $10,200 after a year, but if the price of houses has just gone up by 8%, then you are even further away from homeownership than you were a year ago. However, it looks like you have more money, but you have less when valued against tangible assets.

For this reason, people are looking for alternatives, not because people have something against banks (although many in the crypto world do), it's because they can feel the price of assets running away from them. They are looking to the crypto world with its massive growth as a place for at least securing, if not growing, their wealth at a pace to keep up with the destruction of purchasing power of traditional currencies.

Especially as now, the government printing presses have gone into overdrive mode, some even predicting a colossal crash of traditional currencies (or just eternal inflation). Even if you're not in that doomsday camp, it's fair to say, at the very least, the value of assets priced in dollars and other government-backed currencies have been growing and will continue to grow faster than your pay-check. Crypto is in a unique position to be an asset class that is not only benefiting from all the money printing that is going on but is also an asset class that your average joe can get into very quickly. What's even better is that crypto is outperforming all other asset classes, whether real estate, stocks, precious metals etc.

One of the most popular ways to try and get ahead of inflation is by trading, but as we know from years of running this experiment in crypto, the average retail trader, on the whole, loses money and the ones who do make money get that money from the ones who lost. Some could argue that the monetary policy of printing money to fund government spending has set people's conditions to take more considerable risks as they see the prices of assets racing away. Even if one manages to get ahead with trading, the buying and selling of coins add no real value to society. It's people who have made smarter/luckier bets that win in that game, but as Elon Musk says, 'if nobody makes anything, there are no things'. There are better ways to make your wealth grow without having to risk it all on stocks or the next 'pumping' cryptocurrency.

DeFi aims to create financial products that don't rely on gambling in the crypto exchanges with one coin or another. It treats cryptocurrency as real money and is as serious in the business of money as the traditional banking sector is. People are already earning reasonable interest rates safely in many other ways mentioned before using stable coins. Cryptocurrencies and DeFi are taking away the services that the financial sector used to have a monopoly. One of these services are certificates of deposit (sometimes known as time deposits), and it is this service that Hex is the first crypto alternative.

PRE KNOWLEDGE CHECK

A great teacher of mine once said that you have to go over the previous related topic before starting a new one. In danger of sounding condescending as I assume you, the reader, will be familiar with cryptocurrencies and the blockchain. I feel it best to cover all bases before diving headfirst into the exciting but sometimes dizzying world of Hex and DeFi.

Bitcoin

A coin that needs no introduction, but here is one anyway.

The world's first cryptocurrency, invented in 2009 by a cryptographer going under the alias Satoshi Nakamoto. Since its inception, a single

Bitcoin has gone up in price by a factor of 6 million (as of 2021).

Bitcoin started the revolution in trustless, immutable, distributed peer to peer digital currency. It started out being worth almost nothing and over its first ten years reached a value of $300 Billion. In 2021 it is used more as a store of value and speculative instrument than a day to day currency.

Bitcoin's inflation rate is currently at 1.76% (it was initially 100% per year but has reduced over the years), that inflation gets paid to the miners as a reward for securing the network.

Bitcoin uses 'proof of work' to secure the network, which uses masses of energy and has only gotten worse since the introduction of ASIC mining equipment. A consequence of ASIC mining is that the miners are becoming more centralised as the bar to entry is so high that only some of the most expensive computers situated in places with low energy prices can turn a profit mining Bitcoin. The Bitcoin that miners earn generally gets liquidated to pay for the costs of energy and equipment. Miners selling all of Bitcoin's inflation to pay these costs can harm the price.

Nakamoto disappeared in 2011 and hasn't been

heard from since. His Bitcoin wallet address has around 1.1 million untouched Bitcoins in it.

Ethereum

Developed in 2015 by Vitalik Buterin, a Russian-Canadian computer programmer, Ethereum has managed to hush its naysayers and has proved to be an excellent platform for people to develop projects on a blockchain. It was the first to popularise contracts on a blockchain, known as a smart contract, which instead of using the ledger of a blockchain to hold values of a currency, stores contracts instead. Ethereum has moved away from ASIC mining, and while still using proof of work to secure the network, Ethereum 2.0 is making moves toward 'proof of stake', which requires no miners, it is currently in its beta stage, and as of yet, there has been no confirmed release date. The price of an Ethereum token has gone up over 800,000x since its inception. A token for a project that uses the Ethereum network is called an ERC-20 token.

The Etheruem of 2016 is undoubtedly not the Etheruem of today. That is one of the advantages of having its creator take ownership of the network's problems and making strides in solving them. Unlike

Bitcoin, it has a bug bounty program that can resolve things like inflation bugs and other software issues.

Mining

Mining is how many cryptocurrencies inflate their supply and are a large part of securing a network. Miners get coins by completing 'blocks' of verified transactions; the reward paid for that work are the tokens of that network.

Proof of Work/Proof of Stake

A common way that blockchains secure the network without a third party is through a mechanism called 'proof of work'. To be able to mine blocks and verify transactions, miners have to solve complicated mathematical problems. The problems get more complex as more processing power is added to the network, making it a robust security model. It simply means that no one in the world has enough processing power to take down the network. The downside is that machines are working overtime and burning vast amounts of electricity to solve arbitrary mathematical puzzles (which most of the time they won't be the one to solve). The energy/environmental cost is needed to protect what is now an industry in the trillions of dollars. There is an alternative, a newer method of securing blockchains without miners, proof of stake.

Proof of stake uses the number of tokens someone has to secure the network, based on the idea that the people with the largest 'stake' in that currency have the most substantial incentive to protect the network's integrity. Any wannabe attacker would have to own a significant amount of the supply to be in a position to verify transactions incorrectly. As they accumulated a more substantial stake, the token price would increase, wiping out any economic incentive to compromise a network that they have used a considerable amount of money to acquire. It's a model other currencies have begun to adopt and has had a long enough track record to show it as an effective security model.

Gas

Gas is the cost of doing business on the Ethereum network, paid in Ethereum on every transaction, whether it's moving Ethereum, swapping ERC-20 tokens or using any of the functions of the applications built on Ethereum. Everything needs a little bit of computational power, and in a free market, nothing is for free. Gas prices can vary based upon how much traffic the network has and how much computation your transaction needs.

Roadmap

A Roadmap is where a development team lays out the project's plans; it will usually have expected completion dates for the different development stages.

Forking

When changes happen to a blockchain's protocol, this is known as a fork. A hard fork is where the current infrastructure won't accept the new protocol. When this happens, a split occurs, resulting in a new chain. A soft fork is where the protocol changes are compatible with the current node/mining infrastructure. Ethereum is a hard fork of Etheruem Classic; Bitcoin Cash is a hard fork from the Bitcoin chain. As most blockchain code is open source, anyone with the technical know-how can fork a network. The more challenging part is getting the nodes, miners and users to accept the fork.

Inflation

For this book's purposes, the term inflation refers only to an increase of a currency's supply, not inflation in the sense of rising prices (which currency supply inflation can inadvertently cause).

Certificate of Deposits

A certificate of deposit (a CD) is a product offered by banks and credit unions that provides a high-interest rate in exchange for the customer agreeing to leave a lump sum untouched for a predetermined time. They are among the most popular products that banks offer, and almost all consumer financial institutions provide them. CD terms differ from product to product, but in principle, they work the same, a higher interest rate dependent upon the length of time served on that deposit.

Different financial institutions offer a wide range of rates. Your traditional bank may pay a small amount of interest on even long-term CDs, while an online bank or local credit union might pay three to five times the national average. Meanwhile, some of the best rates come from special promotions, occasionally with unusual durations such as 13 or 21 months, rather than the more common terms based on 3, 6, or 18 months or full-year increments.

CD's are one of the most popular financial products in the market. The amount of CD's worth under $100,000 is a $571 billion market alone. Looking at some advertised rates for CD's and the average example offered an interest rate of 0.5% APY (Annual Percentage Yield) for one year, 2.05% for three years or 2.15% for five years. I know not vast amounts of yield, but it's one of the better deals if you are looking for a safe higher interest in a time of such low interest rates.

INTRODUCTION

I've bought a lot of altcoins, all tied to all sorts of weird and wonderful projects. Whether it's the next 'Ethereum killer', a token for a decentralised power grid, or one to smooth out supply chains, I even have a coin that gives me part ownership of an asteroid.

One of the noticeable things when looking at all of these projects is that you can put them into two categories, projects the market is using today or promises. EOS would only be an 'Ethereum killer' if the developers moved off Ethereum and onto its platform. Coins are just like businesses; most fail. All coins pump in price at some point, but no matter how much the price has mooned or what incredible things they have on their roadmap, their actual value comes once their project is solving an existing problem the market has, not just ballooning in price (for a day).

You may have heard of Bitconnect (a bullet I hoped you managed to dodge), the now cliche word for crypto scams and people losing money. But few have stopped to wonder why a significant number of people bought into Bitconnect, why they happily put their life savings at risk. Two main reasons, Bitconnect was not a promise, and it was paying yield. It was paying out what it said it would and seemed to be fully operational until the end. We all know how the story ended, a website mysteriously turned off, a shiller's fall from grace and a lot of lost wealth.

You either win, or you learn. Bitconnect taught us how crucial earning money on your money is to the market. It also taught us that you should never hand your wealth over to a third party, especially not in crypto. Only you should have your private keys, not unless you want to end up like the unfortunate 'Bitconnectors'?

People will always be looking for ways to get a yield on their capital. Even with the current bull market that we find ourselves in, and everything looks like it's going up and to the right, people will always want to earn interest. A coin can go up in value, but to realise some of that value, you have to sell that coin and all the future potential price appreciation that coin may have. A significant number of people would rather spend interest earned from that coin without breaking into their hard-earned principal.

With this in mind, What is DeFi? aims to have a deeper look at projects that are not a promise but are being used today for their intended purpose. This series is not a look at coins that could potentially 100x your money; there are plenty of people who will tell you all about them. It's about sensible investing with products that already have a tried and tested market fit in the traditional financial sector that has made its way to the world of cryptocurrencies and blockchains.

Hex is a curious case in the crypto sphere for many reasons; you will not see it featured in the Coin Market Cap Top 100, though consistently valued in the top 20 on other listing sites. It's not talked about a lot by the altcoin shillers, traders or pump and dump groups. I see it as an anomaly in the world of DeFi, operating on its own, quietly doing its thing with a community that has been reaping the benefits.

But true to the spirit of What is DeFi?, Hex is a

decentralised financial product aiming to replace one of the traditional financial services (namely, Certificates of Deposit) with a crypto alternative. It's working today, doing the job it was programmed for, and that's what piqued my interest.

CURRENT STATE OF PLAY

BITCOIN VS STABLECOINS VS ALTCOINS

T here are thousands of cryptocurrencies out there, each with a whole host of people telling you that it's the next big thing. Anyone who has ventured even slightly away from Bitcoin and Etheruem will be familiar with the YouTube coin shillers and their ridiculous thumbnails (usually with a rocket and moon in there somewhere).

The question in my mind is, do these coins serve a genuine need in the market? Is something else already doing that job? In the case of DeFi, what financial service is it seeking to replace? The major paradigm shift from traditional finance/business to DeFi is that one project will not replace the services banks currently offer. It will be a mixture of projects, each specialised in that particular service.

In the next chapter, we will briefly look at what I see as the main serious options currently in crypto, what services they fulfil, and what could go wrong with them. All of these cryptos have amazing things going for them, but when thinking, 'Why Hex?' It's good to know where the gap is in the market and if there is a need for something else in the mix. And while the crypto world is moving quickly and some of the words written will be outdated by the time I've finished typing them, some problems are timeless.

Other issues at the time of writing currently have very few people working toward solving them. Lastly, it is prudent to keep in mind that there will always be factors beyond our current understanding that can turn the tide of events or even end a project in its tracks, the so-called black-swan event.

Bitcoin

As of writing, there is no doubt that Bitcoin is the number one cryptocurrency in the world, so why would you want anything else? Some people don't need anything else (and lots will refuse to have anything else - the proudly named 'maximalists').

The truth is Bitcoin is far from perfect. It wastes a lot of energy and pollutes the environment to secure the network. Mining has been getting more centralised (which is more efficient but weakens censorship resistance) due to high barriers to entry. These things probably won't stop Bitcoin's rise, but some things could.

BITCOIN IS OLD CODE

It would be optimistic at best to think that Satoshi Nakamoto invented the first cryptocurrency and got everything correct the first time. If the average maximalist knew how many near misses Bitcoin has, they may change their 'ist' to 'ish'. Chain rollbacks, internal disputes and inflation bugs (luckily caught in time) Bitcoin has had a history of near misses.

The idea that Bitcoin will 100% be the world's next store of value (and only one at that) is a tough sell when we live in uncertain times and probabilities. Bitcoin started this revolution, and everyone in crypto will always love it for that but sometimes, when the world changes, you've got to update your worldview. The introduction of ASIC mining has made the entry barrier to Bitcoin mining much higher and has caused Bitcoin mining to be an even more wasteful exercise. Some qualified people could solve these things, but they have no incentive. Which programmers are spending their highly in-demand time improving a network without reward? (and in most cases receive ridicule) In this regard, Bitcoin does suffer a little from the "tragedy of the commons".

Nobody solely owns the Bitcoin network, which can have a downside that nobody is willing to take responsibility for that network. My humble suggestion to the billionaires who have been making colossal paper gains on Bitcoin would be to use some of those to support the network responsible for their excellent ROI's. The Bitcoin network needs people investing in it, which at the minute most aren't doing; they hope others will do it, so they don't have to and watch as the value of their bag mysteriously grows. The code hasn't gone through an audit, and there has been no 'Bug Bounty program'. Who knows, if there is not another inflation bug lurking around that could lead to the destruction of the network. Bitcoin, for most, is the crypto gateway. Most people associate Bitcoin with the word cryptocurrency, and for the sake of the whole ecosystem, it needs to be better looked after.

Warren Buffet says 'diversifying is a hedge against ignorance' there are always things we don't know and can never predict.

You've 'missed the boat.'

While the 'final' price of Bitcoin is unknown, what is very unlikely is that the Bitcoin price will increase by a factor of 6 million again. For most, the opportunity to turn $100 into a "Lambo" is over. Bitcoin has given fantastic returns compared to traditional assets, but people want more significant gains in crypto. At the same time, I feel that that's a recipe for disaster for the average person, although I can't deny the truth that people are looking for alternatives to make more incredible wealth in this fast-growing asset class.

If you have a lot of capital, a 10% gain may seem reasonable, some people could live off a 10% ROI a year, but most can't. Most people see that stock prices, houses, and other appreciating assets are increasing at a rate out of their grasp and see crypto as a way of keeping up with those price increases. The consensus is that Bitcoin does not offer crazy returns for those kinds of people, and what ends up happening is that they sell their Bitcoin and try to find a more lucrative coin and get 'wrecked' (rekt) by trading altcoins and stocks of companies that have no market value.

HOLDERS MAKE MONEY

As well as founders, Bitcoin taught us that another class of people could also make excellent ROI. Holders. If you had bought Bitcoin at any point before its all-time high, you would have, at least on paper, made a profit. Bitcoin has been making all-time highs every three years. It does require 'strong hands' and a measure of faith to hang onto your Bitcoin. The term Bitcoin maximalist became popular around the 2017 bull market when people realised that the best option for most was to hold on to your Bitcoin. Not getting taken in by the innumerable number of altcoins, all promising something but very rarely delivering.

Holders secure the price, and the holding mentality stops people, who can't see the long market cycles, from getting hung out to dry when the inevitable dip happens.

. . .

You can't earn interest on Bitcoin without handing over control.

Bitcoin has three main functions, send, receive and mine. If you want to earn interest on your Bitcoin, you have to entrust it to a centralised third party. These third parties are wide open to hacking attacks, fraud, high fees, not to mention your loss of privacy. The industry is so lucrative that these third parties have made more money than Bitcoin's creator (and he/they have 1.1 million Bitcoins).

As already mentioned, Bitconnect taught us that handing over control of your money to a third party is a bad idea. It also taught that people want to earn a yield on their investments and are willing to lose everything to do it.

Exchanges offer staking on certain coins in exchange for interest, but as long as your coins are on the exchange, they aren't your coins. Exchanges get hacked, as the Mount Gox trustees know full well. Exchange staking makes me feel a little uneasy. Even though it offers good returns, it has a fractional reserve banking feel to it. They can sell more coins than they have, knowing they have a reserve that will never leave. This practice that is known to devalue currencies is something that blockchains came to abolish.

Bitcoin maximalists and others may not feel that it's that important to be able to earn interest from your cryptocurrency and that you can realise your gains from selling a piece of your bag. Still, as was shown with Bitconnect and countless other products now available, it's clear many people in the world want interest and are willing to risk a lot to get it.

'If the Bitcoin price goes up, why do we need interest?' they say. You can understand the sentiment, but if you want to turn those 'paper gains' into a currency you can buy things with, you have to end up with less Bitcoin at the end of it. Most people don't want that. We all know the story of the pizza bought in Bitcoin that would be worth millions today. People have worked hard to acquire that Bitcoin; they may even plan to retire on that Bitcoin. It seems like if you're holding Bitcoin, you have two choices, lose some of it to realise your paper gains or hang on to it until it becomes a functional currency.

But imagine you could earn interest in Bitcoin? Most people would most likely trade and spend some of the gains made from interest instead of spending Bitcoin acquired with their blood, sweat and tears, which could be worth more in the future. What if people who hold could earn interest with Bitcoin and still hang on to their private keys. As mentioned previously, exchanges are starting to offer 'staking' of Bitcoin for interest, but that means keeping it on an exchange and handing over the control of your money to them. One of the purposes of Bitcoin was to get rid of third parties. You have to trust the exchange that stores your wealth with a coin designed to be trustless.

Key Takeaway

- You can't earn interest with Bitcoin without giving over control of your Bitcoin.
- Bitcoin has had a few bugs and a few near misses (thanks to the Bitcoin Cash developer who spotted it and saved Bitcoin and the wealth of everyone who holds it).
- The Bitcoin price won't go up by 6 million times again.
- The Bitcoin supply inflation goes to the miners who use that Bitcoin to pay for high electricity fees (and lower the price of Bitcoin by selling).

Stable Coins

Stable coins are backed by a reserve asset, resulting in much less volatile currencies and much safer to make financial products.

Stable coins like DAI/Tether etc., have services that offer interest yielding investments. Because they have a peg to the dollar, they have a level of stability, although subject to the same inflation forces as the paper/government-backed currencies are. At the time of writing, the average yield from a stable coin investment is around 7% APY. It is pretty good, probably better than your traditional savings account, even with the extra costs of transacting on the blockchain.

One of the more popular ways to earn yield from stable coins is to add them to a decentralised exchange's liquidity pool. You receive a percentage of the fees from people using that exchange to swap one currency for another. Other platforms lend your coins out and give you a portion of the interest. At the time of writing, stable coins seem to be one of the best ways to 'safely' earn interest, and the price stability puts a lot of minds at ease when deciding to use DeFi to store and grow their wealth.

While the feature of stability is attractive to

some, it is also one of its downsides. People get into crypto because it is the fastest-growing asset class, outperforming things like stocks and real estate. Having it pegged to something they are trying to get away from seems counterproductive to some. Stable coins have their place (another book in the series is on the topic), but as mentioned before, there is not one coin that can solve all the problems in the market.

In a lot of cases, you will be dealing with a third party at some point. Other stable coins have only one point of failure (e.g. they may only have one centrally located server), and with others, you are handing over the control of your wealth, again not precisely 'trustless'.

While an average of 7% APY is excellent for some people, for many others who live paycheck to paycheck or are in similar financial circumstances, 7% is not enough. They want crypto gains that will make a difference in their life (they've seen the Lambo's). They will risk a lot to try and find the 'next Bitcoin'...

KEY TAKEAWAY

- Can earn a higher average interest rate than traditional bank savings account at averaging 7% at the time of writing.
- A lot of the stable coins are centrally controlled currencies or have a single point of attack for hackers.
- Subject to inflation if backed by a fiat currency.
- Much less volatile due to being backed by an asset.

Altcoins

This composite word has lost more people money in crypto than people losing their private keys. Attracted by the promise of 'mad gains', many people go from Bitcoin and Ethereum where they were making decent paper gains and head into the Wild West of the crypto world...the altcoin market.

I'm not saying all altcoins are terrible (with so many out there, it's impossible to make that sweeping judgement), but most have the same things in common. Most are a promise of something coming on the way. With all their teams of people, whitepapers and roadmaps, they promise that if this and this goes their way, you could have just found a gem.

Will they go up, will they go down? Will they be the next Bitcoin? Who knows? Nobody does. But many people profit telling you that they do know. These 'shillers' usually have a big bag of coins themselves and want it to grow, so they tell you it's going to grow. What usually happens is the price pumps, and then because most people aren't traders, they hold on, not having the discipline to sell at the top and then it dumps on their head, and they are left holding a bag of nothing. And because they had no faith in the project, they sell the bottom making huge losses and then try the whole thing again.

I can tell you this first hand as I rode the wave of insanity that was the altcoin season of 2017. At that point, I hadn't learnt this fundamental lesson. There were new coins every week, all offering ICO's (Initial Coin Offerings, new currencies at a 'low' price to start supply). I felt like I was some angel investor of these soon to be giant companies/coins. It didn't quite pan out that way.

Some of you reading this may also have been part of the 'class of 2017'. A baptism by fire for some, but others, many lessons learnt. The current 2021 bull run is a different climate from 2017. Different kinds of investors getting involved, a pandemic and a lot more informed users, but the lessons are there for all who listened in 2017/18. You wouldn't bet on random penny stocks, so why do the same with altcoins? Most people lose money.

If it's a promise of something, you have no idea/control of whether it will work or even if it will get finished, and more times than not, promises get broken.

How many Amazon-like stores were there before the dot.com crash? Who knows? They died. In my own experience with altcoins, lots of them have great ideas, lots of them with great teams, lots of them with a sensible road map but lots of them blow up, and lots of them go to practically zero.

My personal altcoin story was EOS, the next 'Ethereum Killer'. The project made sense in so many ways as it solved many of the problems that Bitcoin and Ethereum had at the time. It had a very experienced blockchain developer in Dan Larimer leading the project, who had already proved himself with his earlier projects, Bitshares and Steemit, both working blockchains still up and running today. It raised billions of dollars through its very well thought out ICO. When the token launched properly, the EOS team offered 1 billion dollars to developers to develop apps on the network. It used a variation of the much more environmentally friendly proof of stake security model. It had paid it's fines to the SEC (the body that regulates crypto and stocks in the US), so no legal troubles. What could go wrong?

The market brah...

I didn't understand the first-mover advantage. I didn't realise that something technically better could still not be the winner (VHS vs Betamax in the videotape wars comes to mind). I didn't understand all of the innumerable factors that could and would cause EOS to fail (some would say just for now). Nobody developed on it. Not even a billion dollars could get any decent projects that the market wanted. Be at one with your ignorance. The people who got in early on Bitcoin are the exception, not the rule. It was a promise, it wasn't a scam, but with all the good intentions in the world, I could do nothing but watch a big part of my hard-earned savings disappear. That experience turned me into a Bitcoin maximalist for a time.

You can't say these things about Bitcoin and Ethereum. Bitcoin is not a promise of a store of value. Etheruem is not a token that someday will have smart contracts developed on it. People are using it for that purpose today. Unlike many copycat projects, the first-mover advantage carries a lot more weight than technical prowess, Ethereum got better, and it's still number one in what it does.

Key Takeaway

- Huge gains to be made but also huge losses (most likely)
- Look for coins that are working now, not just a promise
- The runaway inflation of traditional assets has made people do risky things to keep up.
- Traders (apart from perhaps in a marketing sense if they shill a good coin) add no real value to society.

So what's left? We can see people want interest. People need censorship resistance and control of their own money. People wish to have a chance of mad gains. People want something that is working today and not a promise. Is there a project that can deliver?

2

WHAT IS HEX?

A fter all this trash talk about altcoins, why on earth is a book written about Hex? (which itself is technically an altcoin). Good question. One of the reasons that Hex satisfies my criteria for a DeFi product is that it solves a problem currently in the market, and people are using it for its designed purpose. Hex is a finished product. The code audited and completed, it's working, and people are using it for its intended purpose today.

You can go very deep into the topic of what Hex is and how it does what it does, but for clarity, I'll explain what Hex does and how without too many of the technical details. If you want to explore Hex deeper after reading this section, there is a lot more of the technical information in the 'Technical Stuff' chapter. For those of you who want to go deeper, you can visit an extensive FAQ section on hex.com. There is also a Hex Telegram channel where you can ask any questions to the community. There you'll meet people that will tell you everything there is possibly to know about Hex. I will use current statistics where needed, knowing full well that many of these words will be outdated by the time I've pressed the full stop to this sentence.

Hex is a cryptocurrency that enables you to lock away your wealth for a set amount of time (1 day to 15 years). In exchange for 'staking' coins out of supply and thus helping to secure the price, stakers get paid a share of the currency inflation (delivered daily) plus a percentage of the fees incurred from people who end their stakes early.

Hex is what you would expect from a decentralised financial product.

- Open Source (anyone can develop on Hex and see all the transactions on Hex)
- Trustless (No third party, just you and the smart contract)
- Store of Value (The price has risen over 400x since inception over a year ago)

- Censorship Resistant (anyone can transact on the network provided they follow the predetermined rules of the network protocol)
- Permissionless (can be used without permission from anybody)
- Immutable (the smart contract is set in stone, it cannot be changed, not even by the creator)

Founded by serial entrepreneur and ex-Bitcoin maximalist Richard Heart (the project was initially called Bitcoin Hex), Hex was completed and then launched on December 2nd 2019, as the first decentralised Certificate of Deposit on the Blockchain. Its launch was delayed for almost a year after going through two security audits and one economics audit. Hex launched as a finished product, and because there is no expectation of others' work, it is not classed as a security by the SEC. Hex has no admin keys, no off switch; it is fully autonomous.

It's currently on the Ethereum network and has over $2 billion of wealth already staked and over 100,000 wallets using it (with 30,000 of those being stakers). The average stake length is presently more than five years and growing with 10-year stakes making close to 40% APY. Due to its decentralised nature, all the stakes, current supply and payouts are viewable to anyone who wants to see them. There is also a project soon to be released that will give Hex users an alternative to the Ethereum chain if they wish.

In its initial phase, Hex's tokens were given free to Bitcoin holders who had a year to claim (that period is over). One of the most significant claims staked their Hex for 15 years on Day 1. After that initial period, any unclaimed Hex was then distributed amongst the people who had claimed.

Since then, it has seen a massive price increase, going from being worth 1 Satoshi (100 millionths of a Bitcoin) to worth around 5 cents. I usually don't like using price as the primary metric for success, as I risk sounding like a typical altcoin 'shiller'. But its consistent price increase is a good indication that people are using it and are happy with its service. It has also made appearances as a top 10 cryptocurrency on listing sites like nomics.com and coinranking.com.

How Much Interest Can I Earn?

The longer you stake, the more you make.

It would be nice to say you earn such an amount of interest per year in Hex, but your stake's length and size are significant factors to your APY (annual percentage yield). At the moment, longer stakes pay, on average, around 36.9% APY. The general interest rate across all stakes, long and short, is about 13% APY. This number can change daily (but not hugely) as people who are starting/ending their stakes also changes daily.

The percentage of total Hex staked determines the amount of daily interest the smart contract delivers.

100% of Hex staked = 3.69% APY
10% of Hex staked = 36.9% APY
1% of Hex staked = 369% APY

Like a traditional CD, you get a higher interest rate the longer you lock up your wealth. Every extra year staked in Hex, stakers receive an additional 20% in interest rate (a typical traditional CD rate).

Where does the Interest come from?

Every year the total Hex supply inflates by a maximum of 3.69%. That extra Hex supply gets paid to the people who have their wealth staked in Hex, also known as the 'staker class'. Stakers also receive 50% of the fees from people who end their stakes early.

Many people wonder how the price can go up even as supply increases. Remember that Bitcoin's inflation rate was much higher than that for around ten years (on its way to $20,000). Still, the price of Bitcoin increased due to the number of users outweighing the amount it inflates. Bitcoin pays its inflation to the miners, who sell it to pay for the costs of running a mining operation.

In Hex, inflation is paid to the stakers and doesn't come back into supply until a stake has ended. At the minute, the average stake is around five years, so a lot of that inflation won't even happen until years down the line. Hex also has a mechanism to ensure that much of that inflation never enters supply, more on that to come.

How do I get Rewarded for Staking Longer?

Your interest gets paid in Hex. What decides how much interest you receive are the shares known as T-shares (T for trillion). You buy T-shares with Hex; the longer you stake, the extra amount of T-shares you receive (20% a year, maxing out after ten years). The T-share idea is the more complicated and unique part of the Hex contract, we will go deeper into T-shares in a later chapter, but I'll use an example to shine a light on it for now.

EXAMPLE

- You buy 10,000 Hex (this is your principal)
- You decide to stake for ten years (20% extra Hex added for each year) that gives you an extra 20,000 Hex.
- Your 'effective Hex' is 30,000; this is what determines how many T-shares you receive.
- If the T share price is 15,000 Hex, the contract will record you as having 10,000 Hex principal and 2 T-shares

- Now for the slightly tricky bit. As your daily interest is paid per T-share, not based on your principal, someone with 2 T-shares and a 10,000 Hex principal would receive the same amount of daily interest as someone with 30,000 and 2 T-shares.

Because your APY is your interest divided by your principal, the person with 10,000 Hex and two T-shares will get a higher percentage return. For someone to have the same amount of T-shares but a higher principal, they either staked for a shorter amount of time or started their stake much later.

The T-share price is constantly increasing (in terms of Hex), so you will never be able to buy a T-share for the same price you bought in the past (not without staking longer). The T-share mechanism is one of the ways that some of the inflation gets burned. Once people have ended their stake, many will take some of the gains and re-stake the rest. Due to a higher T-share price than bought initially, that price difference will effectively remove that Hex from supply permanently.

In layman's terms, longer staking increases your daily interest payment.

You also get a smaller reward based on the size of your stake. You can receive up to a 10% bonus (capped at 150 million Hex) for increasing the size of your stake, but it's fair to say that the length of your stake will increase your ROI more than the size of it.

The interest in Hex is not compounding interest as you would have at a bank, but if the Hex price rises in dollars, your principal and interest also increase when measured against dollars. The Hex price more than tripled in the early half of 2021 alone.

We will look at T-shares in-depth in a later chapter. For now, as long as we know that T-shares are how Hex pays interest and distributes penalties.

Receiving Penalties

Not only do stakers receive Hex's inflation, but they also receive the penalties from others who have ended their stake early.

When you stake your Hex, you are signing a smart contract. You have agreed to stake your Hex for an agreed period in exchange for more T-shares and, therefore, higher interest. The contact will trustlessly keep its end of the bargain if you keep up yours. So what if you want to end your stake early?

You can 'emergency' end your stake in Hex, but not without a penalty. If you were to end your stake exactly halfway through your term, you would get the principal back but none of the interest. If you terminate your stake earlier, you will lose a percentage of the principal in proportion to the time served. Half of all these penalties go to the existing stakeholders, who were staked on the same day.

The other half of the penalties go to the Origin address (see Chapter 5). The percentage of T-shares you have at that point will decide how much of the fee you receive.

There is also a penalty for not ending a stake once it has served its term. You have 14 days to complete the stake once it's matured. After that, fees charge 1% of the stake per week (known as bleeding out). These fees are an incentive for people to end their stakes on time. The reason being that as long as your stake hasn't ended, your T-shares are still in supply, and that will reduce other people's rewards.

Where does Hex get its Value?

Hex is a cryptocurrency that allows you to lock up your wealth and pays a high level of interest in Hex, but where does Hex derive its value? It's no good getting paid interest in Hex if, after my stake ends, the Hex is worth less than when I initially staked?

People give things their value. You may hear the word 'intrinsic value' when people talk about things like gold but what intrinsic value means is consensus. There is a large consensus in the world that believe that gold has value. Of course, gold has specific properties that lend themselves to having that consensus. It's pretty, it's rare, it doesn't tarnish. It has lots of properties that make it a good store of value, but if everyone decided tomorrow, gold was a useless yellow metal worth nothing, it would be worth nothing. If it had actual intrinsic value, how come you don't see baboons hoarding stacks of gold and fighting over them?

Hex the token is a cryptocurrency like any other. If nobody uses it, then it's worthless, just like Bitcoin. People buying and others selling are what makes price move. Does Hex have any characteristics that would give it a consensus? Does Hex address some of the gaps in the DeFi and cryptocurrency market? A market where there is already a consensus of millions.

Earning Yield without Relinquishing Control.

As mentioned before, the story of Bitconnect and countless others show demand for interest-earning investments in crypto. The explosion of the stable coins used on lending platforms and liquidity pools shows there are functioning, price secure, yield giving investments on a blockchain. However, most of these coins have a third party somewhere along the line. That could be the platform itself or a central party that owns even the network. Hex allows you to make high interest on your crypto with the bonus of price appreciation and no third parties. Only you are in control of your private keys, and you mint your coins. It runs without any third party, meaning there is no risk of ending up like those poor folks invested in Bitconnect. One day they logged in and realised that their money wasn't their money anymore.

Hex Saves you from Yourself.

All those people who sold Bitcoin at 1¢, $1,000 or even $20,000 are generally kicking themselves right now. If only they'd had more faith that the price would keep going up and to the right. If only they could have weathered the 3-year cycles of bear and bull markets. That's the nature of most people, myself included. That's why most of us get wrecked on the financial markets. We are too easily lured in and then shook out. With Hex, once you've staked, you're in it for the long haul. Those day-to-day price fluctuations start to matter less, and there is nothing you could do even if the price exploded. You are unable to get FOMO and sell all your Hex for the next shiny object. You wait, that's all you do, what could you do in the meantime, now you don't need to stare at charts? Something productive, maybe go out into the world and create real value while your stakes mature. To have a stake that won't mature until the future takes away all those temptations that the crypto world can offer and can teach a great lesson in delayed gratification.

In Bitcoin, Bitcoin holders are, in essence, stakers, if not by the noun, then certainly by the verb. Their refusal to sell is what secures the Bitcoin price and why it's a good sign when Elon Musk and other billionaires are getting into Bitcoin (although things are constantly changing) and saying that they will never sell. The stakers in Hex are the ultimate holders. They can't sell, so the price is secured, with the only difference being that the inflation of Bitcoin goes to the miners who secure the network, not to the holders who secure the price.

Traders Gonna Trade

Love it or hate it, one of crypto's actual use cases is in trading. For the most part, it's legalised gambling, but there is a lot of economic activity in it. There are opportunities to get some of that economic activity. Lending platforms where you can earn yield, lending your wealth to traders who use it as collateral for their actions and paying you some interest. It's similar in Hex. Plenty of people don't stake Hex, and they trade with it. Weirdly, because only stakers receive the inflation, the people who deal in Hex borrow its value from the stakers who receive the rewards.

No matter how much you warn people, no matter how much you tell them that trading adds no value to society, people will trade. Especially now, with asset prices running away from the working and middle classes, they look for ways of growing their wealth faster than the inflation of real estate, stocks, and other 'rich people' assets. Someone with a small amount of capital can't keep up in this current climate without doing something risky like trading.

Most people who trade most likely lose; anyone who bought Bitcoin and sold it has most likely lost. It doesn't have to be that way.

Hex is an alternative way to grow your investments in crypto without trading or handing over your private keys to someone else. You get the chance to have a newer coin that can appreciate an order of magnitude in price and benefit from earning yield on top. Even if Hex's price stagnated and didn't move, you would still get the interest made. Is not losing all your money trading a value proposition? What if the people who bought Bitcoin in 2011 weren't allowed to touch it for ten years without penalty? Do you think they would have done better or worse if they had been unable to trade it?

3

HOW DO I GET HEX?

As of writing, the easiest currency to trade for Hex is Ethereum. (although other coins like stable coin USDC are becoming highly liquid). You will need some Ethereum not only to buy Hex but also to fund the staking. To do anything on the Ethereum network, you need to pay the gas. You pay gas with 'Eth', so having some lying around your wallet is never a bad idea.

Admittedly, it takes slightly longer to buy Hex than just buying some Bitcoin. Each step is not difficult, even if there are more than usual. There are a few ways to buy/stake/store Hex, but I'll go through the most common way for ease. You will need.

- Ethereum
- A Metamask wallet (Chrome and Brave, among others, support this)

Once that is set up, transfer your Ethereum to your Metamask wallet.

Metamask

Once you have your Ethereum (from whichever exchange you use, Kraken, Coinbase etc.), you need to turn it into Hex. Metamask is an Ethereum wallet that specialises in converting Ethereum into the ERC-20 tokens (an ERC-20 is a token on the ethereum network). It hosts several working blockchains, but by far, the Ethereum chain is the most popular.

Metamask is a browser extension that works on many popular browsers. Important. Once you have created a wallet, make sure you store those 12 seed words offline. Don't ever give your seed words out.

Transfer your Ethereum to your Metamask wallet and then use ethhex.com to swap it for Hex. Pay the gas (again). Now you have Hex in your Metamask wallet. You can also direct swap in Metamax, but you will most likely get a better price on ethhex.com. Ethhex.com connects to your Meta-mask wallet to make the exchange.

Stake

You don't have to stake your Hex, but unstaked coins don't receive any inflation/fees that staked coins do. A vast majority of people don't stake. There are many reasons for this. Perhaps high 'gas' prices would undo any short term gains made or holding Hex for price appreciating purposes only. Hex can be left in your Metamask wallet and converted back to Ethereum if needed. But if you want to do what Hex was designed for then, you stake them.

Go to go.hex.com and then click the 'Stake' tab at the top. This will bring you to the staking page. Your Metamask wallet should automatically connect (login into Metamask if it doesn't), and your Hex balance will show as available.

Courtesy of go.hex.com

Here you choose how much you want to stake and for how long. Ten years (3651 days) is the last time you get the 'Longer Pays Better' bonus T-shares. The longest stake is 5555 days (around 15 years). People who take these stakes get inducted into the '5555 club'.

Once your length and amount are chosen, hit start stake, pay the gas and hey presto, your stake has begun. Your stake begins the following day, and that's when you will see how much interest is accruing etc.

At this point, only two things matter, al a The Wire "the day you get in, and the day you get out". There is no more need to be spending your days looking at charts trying to catch the dip and sell the top. Until your stake ends, even if the price moons, there is nothing you can do (without severe penalty) if the price tanks the same. All that matters is how much your Hex is worth the day your stake ends. But if you're like most, you'll probably still look at the chart from time to time.

Ending Stakes

If you decide you need to unstake your coins before your agreed-upon term is over, you can. This is known as an 'Emergency end stake'.

There are many reasons people would end their stake early. Perhaps a change in the financial situation means they want cash quick, or maybe they were involved in the free claim period and had made such a profit already they could take the penalties and still make a profit.

This, as mentioned in the previous chapter,

comes with a fee. The fee is a percentage of your stake based upon the number of days served/left.

Once you hit the 'End stake' button, the smart contract has some work to do. It needs to work out all the daily payouts you are due from inflation and fees (if you had a long stake, it's a lot of computation), and the gas price will reflect that extra computation. The longer the stake, the higher the gas charge to end the stake. The coins will get minted back into existence and appear back into your Metamask wallet.

As well as the end stake function, you can also use the 'Good Accounting' option, where you can defer the minting of your coins (useful for tax purposes in some territories) and not be charged any of the 'late end stake' fees. You will receive no interest from a stake that is in the 'Good Accounting' state.

One other thing to note is that anybody can put your matured state into a Good Accounting state. This is useful if you can't get to your stakes for whatever reason. Someone else can put it into Good Accounting for you, so you don't incur any fees. Some community angels look out for stakes about to go into late fees and put them into Good Accounting to save them being charged.

Keeping Track of Your Stakes

Now your stake is set, there is nothing much you can do until the term ends, but it's always nice to look to see how it's doing what the current interest rate is and how it's maturing. You can do this through go.hex.com, but some excellent apps that the community have built to make it easier to check on your stakes on the go.

The staker.app is a nicely designed app where you can check your stakes and some of the significant movements happening on the network. You can see what percentage of the T-shares you own, how much it would cost to early end stake, and there are mini-leagues, enabling you to see what position you are, compared to all the other stakers.

Stake Ladders

People who save small amounts of money monthly in Hex or people who want to time their end stakes to give an annual/monthly/weekly income in the future will set up what's known as a Stake ladder. The Hex system ensures that you make higher returns having one long stake, but for people on a budget or if you want to time your stakes, you can make them mature at different times. You can do multiple stakes that end at differing times. There is no limit to the number of stakes you can place. Each one will cost gas to start, and you will pay more overall in gas charges for multiple end staking, but it is a great way to give your future self a constant incremental payday. There are many ways to set up your ladder and plenty of YouTube videos outlining all the different variations.

You can also view when other people stakes are maturing. Generally, if lots of stakes mature simultaneously, the Hex price that day will likely be lower. As it can be assumed that that extra 'sell pressure' will lower the price. You can use the website hex.vision and see when other stakes are maturing and time yours on a day without as many, maximising your ROI.

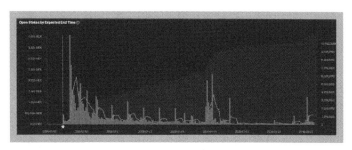

Courtesy of Hex.vision

You can time your stakes to mature on days where others aren't.

4

THE HEX COMMUNITY

Richard Heart

I t's hard to write a book on Hex without a small mention of its inventor Richard Heart. A former Bitcoin maximalist and serial entrepreneur, he was mining Bitcoin in the good old days when one person could get a 50 Bitcoin block reward using a CPU.

Retired at 23, after setting up a whole host of businesses (everything from SEO to mortgage brokering), he started up a YouTube channel giving people advice on starting businesses, improving their social skills (among many other topics). Max Keiser (one of the worlds most famous maximalists) called on him to speak about the Bitcoin/Bitcoin Cash split on his show 'The Keiser Report'.

Disillusioned with the Bitcoin community and the direction the developers were going in, he decided to make a cryptocurrency that addressed the software bugs with Bitcoin and some of its economic problems. Originally he wanted to build on the Bitcoin network until he realised that the chain was unusable for any practical applications. After some updates and improvements to Ethereum, he changed his opinion on Etheruem and decided it was a much better platform to develop a cryptocurrency.

He then renounced his Bitcoin maximalism, and while he wishes Bitcoin well (and still has a few Bitcoin's lying around himself), he became more of a supporter of Ethereum and praised the improvements made to the network.

Now that Hex is finished and become a multi-billion dollar cryptocurrency, he's not resting on his laurels. He is currently working on a project, ' Pulse Chain', that addresses some of the problems with the current Ethereum network. These include using proof of stake instead of proof of work to secure the network and handling the astronomical fees Ethereum can have when there is high volume usage.

He hosts regular live streams on YouTube, where

he takes questions from the public, debates with the industry's leading minds, and keeps the community up to date with what is happening with the project and the crypto world. His famed 8 hour live streams, terse style when taking questions from the public and his deep understanding of the world and crypto makes for entertaining and informative viewing. It also gives people particular security when the founder of a token is very public, honest, and easy to contact.

He is an active member of the Hex Telegram channel and will answer questions from time to time and chirp into conversations.

He has authored two books, 'Scivive' and 'How to Fix the World', that he gives away free. Even though he is the founder of Hex, he doesn't 'own' the Hex network. Once the smart contract started, it can't be changed, not even by him. If he died tomorrow (god forbid), the Hex smart contract would go on as if nothing had happened.

The Community

Is there a Bitcoin community? What about a Ripple one? Who is the community of any of these crypto's you hear? The truth is, from where I'm looking, they don't have one. Like many holders of a particular token, Bitcoin holders are disbursed worldwide, mainly focusing on personal things and expecting someone else to do something to make their investment grow. I've never really seen the type of enthusiasm in my comings and goings (unless you count that one guy shouting 'Bitconnect!') than I do from the holders of Hex...the 'Hexicans'.

One look at the Hex Telegram channel, you will see that the Hexicans are a dedicated group from all walks of life, many of whom in their spare time use one of their particular talents to help the Hex ecosystem. Apps developed, songs written, memes created, conferences organised, T-shirts printed, tattoos burned on, talk shows broadcast, full-page ads taken, websites hosted, and new customers serviced. It is impossible to list all the different projects that the Hex community are creating. What's essential is that Hex has a positive community motivated to make the Hex ecosystem strong and thriving.

The fact they have the name 'Hexicans' speaks volumes, I can't remember hearing of a cryptocurrency community having a word, but admittedly, it's not how I spend my free time. They don't quite have a Hex nation, but many have connected in Puerto Rico.

The people in the Hex community have one thing in common. They have a consensus on Hex's value proposition. Many feel Hex has changed their lives. It's fair to say this is a group of people who love Hex. These aren't your average 'fair-weather' community who flee when the price chart starts looking bearish. The general Hexican is die-hard and has such faith in Hex that they look forward to a bear market. They see it as a way to buy a dip.

In the true spirit of a decentralised community, which can seem a little disorderly, they see the value in reducing the supply of something to secure the price. They believe that there are still many people who will in the future believe the same thing. Many went through the 'class of 2017' and watched count-less people get FOMO, sell their coins and get lured into shiny object syndrome when that bull market hit. Then it ended, the price of all coins took a massive hit in 2018, and lots never came back up. It happens all the time. It's human nature. Hex protects them from their own worst enemy, which in the crypto wild west is themselves.

Hex is decentralised, and to avoid being labelled as a security by the SEC, the community of stakers and users must do all the work on Hex. The code is written, audited and finished. What comes after is up to the community. What helps Hex helps the community, as they all have skin in the game. They aren't going anywhere. The average stake length is five years, so lots are using their free time to help the community any way they can.

This list is endless, but unlike lots of coins where no one is ready to take ownership, the community understands they all have a part to play in improving the Hex ecosystem any way they can, based on their talents and expertise. The stakers (like the HODLR's of Bitcoin) hold Hex's value.

People give things their value, and the community in which specific cryptocurrency has is a good indication of how healthy the project is.

You can see what the Hex community is up to at hex.com/community or on the Hex Telegram channel.

5

THE DOWNSIDES

A s stated before, this book is not financial advice, just a deeper dive into one of many cryptocurrencies that people want in this post Bitcoin era. We have talked about the positives to Hex and why people feel it's a worthy investment. To get a clear picture, we need to outline some current and possible problems and never forget to consider our ignorance of possibilities in the future.

Nobody to Blame

In Hex, you - and you alone - control your private keys to your stakes which you receive a yield on every single day. Being in charge of your private keys is an extra responsibility placed on the holder of the currency. If something goes wrong with our bank account, we lose our cards, or we get scammed, the bank can usually sort the mess. With crypto, it's different. Having full ownership of something means you also have complete responsibility for its security. Like Bitcoin or any other cryptocurrency, for that matter, if you lose your private keys (the 12 seed words), you lose your Hex.

Ensure you store those keywords offline, write them down (maybe more than once), and put them somewhere safe. If you want to go one step further, you can delete Metamask and wipe any trace of those keys from your computer.

There are no expectations of future work from others in Hex, no roadmap outlining targets for the project to hit. If you want Hex, for example, to have better marketing, you've got to do it yourself. Many people didn't like the original website, so it was up to someone in the community to build a better one. If Hex doesn't make it, you have nobody else to blame.

The Cost of Doing Business

Cryptocurrency is one of the most accessible markets globally and is a genuinely free market. But in a free market, nothing of worth is for free. You will have to pay fees every step of the way. It's essential to be aware that there is a cost to every transaction made on that network (especially those who set up smaller stakes). There are fees to turn your fiat money into Ethereum, move that Ethereum to a wallet, swap for Hex, stake that Hex, and an even bigger fee when you end your stake. At times, especially recently, the gas fees on the Ethereum network can be very high, wiping out any of the returns from smaller/shorter stakes.

High fees can be offset by exchanging on the weekends and weeknights (US time zones) and setting limit orders to offset the gas prices (although that relies on at least a temporary price dip and patience). Currently, there is still a disadvantage if you are putting in small amounts. At times of high usage, the 'gas' fees can be costly and have to be a factor when calculating your ROI.

These costs could be the thing of the past. Ethereum 2.0, when released, is moving to a proof of stake model, which would heavily reduce the network fees. However, there is no confirmed date for this and for the time being, you are at the mercy of high gas prices. Apart from Ethereum 2.0, the creator of Hex, Richard Heart, is also working on forking the Ethereum network to have Hex run on its ecosystem. 'Pulse Chain' (its current working title) would have a proof of stake model and do away with high fees associated with a proof of work/mining. Pulse Chain is due to be released in 2021 and, as you would expect, has the full backing of the Hex community. The Hex Community has noted that high gas prices are hurting people who have smaller stakes at times, wiping out much of their gains. A solution is coming, but until then, the Ethereum network has high fees.

No Guaranteed Price

Let's say you staked $1000 worth of Hex that you bought for 1 cent each. With this 100,000 Hex, you decide to stake for a year, and you get a 30% APY, plus some of a share of other people's penalties along the way, and get 137,000 Hex. You end your stake, and after paying the gas, it turns out Hex is now worth half a cent each. You then have a choice, half your earnings or re-stake for longer as T-shares' price will have increased since you started your stake. The Hex price is like anything. If people are buying and not selling, it moves up. Once people have staked, those coins are burned and removed from the supply, so if the supply goes down and demand stays static, price increases. But nothing is guaranteed in cryptocurrency. You can offset this by timing your stakes to end when other's don't. Timing your end stake, at least in theory, will mean that Hex is at a higher price when you mint your coins. The website Hex.vision is a community built website where you can see all sorts of data on Hex, including when people are ending their stakes.

Gatekeeping

Due to Hex's unusual model of burning coins and creating T-shares, Hex doesn't appear in the Top 100 of many of the most prominent coin listing sites that base their rankings on an arbitrary market cap. Some have Hex listed in the low 200's even though other sites like nomics.com will consistently have Hex as one of the top 10 - 20 coins. This 'gatekeeping' has led Hex not to have the exposure it would have otherwise gotten. Many traders will buy coins and push the price with nothing more than a coin market cap chart as their guide to buying. Hex at the minute doesn't have that luxury, currently languishing in the rankings with projects that are unheard of and have very little capital in them.

The Origin Address

One of Hex's minor mysteries is the origin address, an Ethereum wallet that received Hex during the free claim period. This wallet also gets the other half of the early end stake fees. Nobody knows who owns this origin wallet, and Richard Heart, the creator of Hex, has mentioned a few times that he can't divulge who or what receives the Hex in the origin address for a few reasons. This could be for legal purposes to ensure Hex doesn't get labelled as a security by the SEC. It could also perhaps be that the people linked to that address want to remain anonymous. If you're pretty well known to have a wallet with lots of coins in, I imagine you would get inundated with people asking for this or that.

I'm not sure the origin is necessarily a downside of Hex, but I feel it would be remiss of me not to mention it. The origin address has no control of the Hex contract itself, that code is set in stone, and nobody, not even its creators, can change it.

6

THE TECHNICAL STUFF

T-shares

Now to have a look at some of the more technical aspects of Hex. We will start with the 'special sauce' of the Hex contract, namely the T-share. Before delving in, I will quickly recap on what we know about T-shares from the previous chapter.

- T-shares decide how much daily interest you receive.
- T-shares are always going up in price (in Hex terms).
- T-shares are what make 'longer pay better' and 'bigger pay better'.

T-shares (short for terra or trillion shares) are the mechanism in which the smart contract distributes interest to the stakers. When you stake your Hex, the Hex gets burned, and T-shares are created (although the smart contract records your principal Hex amount). Each day, a T-share pays out an amount based upon the total amount of T-shares divided by the daily inflation. Fees from 'emergency end stakes' are also paid per T-share. The T-shares, more than the Hex token itself, are what will become more scarce over time.

Hex's inflation is around 63 million Hex per day (3.69% a year) this paid to the stakers. Those 63 million Hex are distributed evenly across all the current T-shares.

There are currently around 11 million T-shares, which works out at approximately 5.5 Hex daily payout per T-share. Now (April 2021), you can get around one T-share if you stake 6000 Hex ($120) for ten years. If this daily payout stays static at around 5.5 a day after a year, you will have earned around 2000 in Hex, which works out at 33.3% APY.

▼ Day	Day Payout Total	T-Shares Total	Payout per T-Share	% Gain	% APY
500	67.039M	11.190M	6.639	0.107%	39.16%
499	63.274M	11.105M	5.796	0.101%	37.04%
498	63.316M	11.097M	5.750	0.102%	37.32%
497	63.858M	11.069M	5.768	0.102%	37.39%
496	64.232M	11.083M	5.794	0.103%	37.62%
495	63.546M	11.079M	5.737	0.101%	37.22%
494	63.085M	11.069M	5.686	0.101%	36.96%
493	63.635M	11.060M	5.748	0.102%	37.36%
492	64.377M	11.024M	5.639	0.103%	37.56%
491	63.257M	11.021M	5.725	0.103%	37.41%
490	63.552M	11.013M	5.770	0.103%	37.64%
489	64.912M	11.009M	5.915	0.104%	38.18%
488	63.915M	11.018M	5.800	0.104%	38.11%
487	65.830M	11.089M	5.962	0.107%	39.11%
486	63.582M	11.063M	5.746	0.102%	37.47%
485	63.662M	11.047M	5.762	0.102%	37.53%

Courtesy of go.hex.com

Here is a snapshot of about 16 days in Hex. We can see the daily payouts are pretty consistent and in line with the total number of T-shares.

If more people stake and create T-shares, then the daily payout goes down, and if more people end their stakes, then the converse is true. One of the more unique things about Hex is that if more people are staking, even though APY in Hex goes down, one can assume that the Hex token price in dollars will go up as more people will be buying Hex to stake. So it's a win-win for a staker.

As mentioned, the T-share price is always going up (how much it goes up depends on the previous day's end stakes) and going up faster than the actual Hex supply is inflating. T-shares become more scarce over time as the amount of T-shares the total Hex supply could buy goes down. This mechanism means that in 10 years, you won't have everyone dumping their coins and killing the price. If they want to re-stake, those people will have to pay a lot more to get the same amount of T-shares they did all those years ago. They won't even be able to buy the same amount even with all the interest and fees accrued over that period. This incentivizes having longer stakes over constantly maturing shorter ones; it also means that the initial stakers will always get a better deal than those who came after. Like all good ideas, the ones who saw the value earlier get a more significant payoff. You can still make great returns on Bitcoin but not as good as you could in the past but better than those who invest later. You can say the same with all successful businesses, Amazon, Google, Facebook etc.

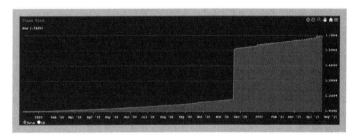

Courtesy of graphex.rocks

This is the T-share price in terms of Hex. That considerable spike was during 'the big payday', which was the end of getting the initial supply of Hex into circulation and when many people sold their stakes to get their free payout. Since that colossal spike, the T-share price has been rising steadily and moving along with the predicted line we can see in the dots.

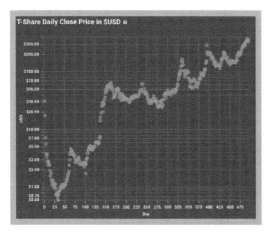

Courtesy of go.hex.com

The T-share price is always going up in terms of Hex. The cost of Hex, however, varies in dollars. It is possible in a Hex price 'dip' to get a T-share for a lower dollar price.

Maximum Number of T-shares

You buy T-shares with Hex, so theoretically, the maximum number of T-shares is all the Hex supply staked for the most extended period (5555 days). It is only theoretical as T-shares are created/burned every day, and the chances that every person who holds Hex stakes it for 15 years is improbable. But thinking about the maximum number of T-shares can help one understand how T-shares are becoming more scarce over time. As the T-share price goes up faster than the inflation, the maximum theoretical amount of T-shares is reducing every day.

If everybody staked all the possible Hex in supply for the maximum amount of time, theoretically, that would be all the T-shares in existence, and everyone would get an APR of 3.69%. If more people stake, thus fewer coins on the market, the price will drive up exponentially. The rapidly moving price would incentivise people to take the hit of an early end stake fee and liquidate their Hex as the profit would quickly compensate for the loss of interest. In doing so, they would be putting Hex back into supply, thus making T-shares available again.

Why T-shares Anyway?

You may be wondering why have T-shares at all? Can't I stake my 10,000 Hex for a set amount of time and get the interest on that. The problem is the initial amount Hex you have is only one factor affecting your principal's amount of interest. Adding time to your stakes gives you a better proportion of T-shares for your principal. Without the T-shares, you wouldn't be able to get the extra benefit from staking your Hex longer.

The T-share also takes into account the fees you are due from others ending their stakes early. One of Hex's value propositions is the time value of money, where the inpatient (who want to end their stakes early or use Hex to trade) pay the patient (who get a share of those early end stake fees and who get the inflation of the currency).

Without a rising T-share price, there wouldn't be a massive benefit to staking once for longer instead of several short stakes. The T-share price going up means that you will not be able to buy T-shares for the same price you when you first staked unless you stake longer or bigger.

Inflation Forever?

All currencies inflate. Bitcoin's initial inflation rate was 100% a year. It has subsequently reduced through each 'halving' (reducing the payment Bitcoin miners receive) down to 1.74% a year. Despite all that inflation, the Bitcoin price still rose as more people saw the utility in it. Bitcoin's inflation rate was higher than Hex's is now until the price reached $20,000. Due to the gap in the market it services, the demand for Bitcoin far outweighs the amount of supply inflation, hence a rising price (Even after 5,000 years gold is still inflating at around 1.5% a year).

The same can be said for Hex as there is a gap in the market for a fully decentralised and interest yielding product. So far, the demand for that has outpaced its inflation. Due to many people ending their stakes and then re-staking, much of Hex's inflation gets burned up (at least in part) to pay for T-shares at a higher price. For the staking class, it's as if the supply doesn't inflate at all due to the reducing amount of T-shares that the total supply can buy.

Today's interest from your bank account is also paid through currency inflation. The way the traditional banking system used to work was that banks would use depositors money to enable them to make loans through fractional reserve banking. That is no longer the case; depositors' money is now used as collateral so commercial banks can borrow money from central banks at a meagre interest rate. This cheap money printed up by the central banks is the

inflation of the currency. A small part of that inflation gets paid to the depositors, the 'holders' if you
will. But Hex's inflation pales in comparison. Two-
thirds of all dollars in existence were created over the
12 months of the Covid-19 pandemic. That's a lot.
Most of this inflation has landed in rich people's
assets, real estate, luxury items, stocks etc. This is
why we have runaway prices in terms of dollars for
those things.

The Ethereum Network

Hex currently runs as an ERC-20 on the Ethereum
network, but it is not tied exclusively to that network.
If it ever got to the point where the Ethereum
network went down or was no longer feasible, Hex
can move to another chain. There are talks of Hex
moving to a new network called 'Pulse Chain', a fork
from the Ethereum network. If it sounds a bit risky
forking the leading smart contract platform on the
blockchain, keep in mind that today's Ethereum is a
fork of Ethereum, now known as Ethereum Classic.
When that chain split, everybody got the new
Ethereum and Ethereum Classic. The new
Ethereum is what the consensus of people call 'the
real one'.

If Hex forks the Ethereum chain, it will have two contacts running side by side. One on the Ethereum network (code set in stone, remember, there will always be Hex on Ethereum) and another on the new chain. Both may have a life of their own, each with their own price discovery, whatever the market decides. Either way, the Hex contract will still be running on both chains, paying out rewards like it always has.

7

THE FUTURE OF HEX

The long term goals of Hex are as lofty as the long term goals of DeFi in general. According to hex.com, this is Hex's ambition.

Replace gold as a store of value (7.7 Trillion USD). Replace credit card companies and payment companies like PayPal (around $770 billion in Visa, MasterCard, and PayPal alone) Replace legacy certificates for deposit ($571 Billion in the USA alone on just those under $100,000) Replace middlemen with trustless interest.

Sounds very ambitious, but many believe that crypto and DeFi will disrupt those sectors massively. There is so much economic energy wasted in the current financial institutions (paying intermediaries) that blockchain technology can offer alternatives without wasting the same money. A smart contract on a blockchain does not need the vast overheads of building and paying go-betweens. DeFi is a much more efficient way of doing financial business, and the industry is only growing.

Hex as a cryptocurrency can do all these things. Hex is a regular currency as well as a mechanism for earning yield. Already some things accept Hex as payment. I feel it won't just be one coin to "rule them all" because of the blockchain's decentralised nature and its users' mentality. It will be a makeup of different currencies replacing the services of an industry worth trillions of dollars. The blockchain is much more efficient than the traditional sectors are, meaning they can compete much easier. DeFi can offer better products with better returns.

Pulse Chain

Currently, Hex is on the Etheruem network, but as the Ethereum network has grown in popularity, its cost has also risen. High gas costs have been a problem for Hex users, especially those with smaller, shorter stakes, who have their gains eaten up by gas fees. To solve this, Richard Heart and a team are developing 'Pulse Chain', an Ethereum fork that will use proof of stake, eliminating mining costs and considerably reducing fees.

Ethereum 2.0 is also doing something similar, but the release date of that is currently unknown. When the split occurs, what will most likely end up happening is that people will use whatever has the best usability and lower fees. That will be the chain that will become the main chain for Hex.

Once 'Pulse Chain' is complete, I imagine that the Hexicans will stop using the Ethereum contract and move onto this new chain. But the market will ultimately decide. The Etheruem Hex contract will still be there, all the stakes, all the T-shares, all the tokens, but it will be the most used chain that gets the greater price appreciation. It could even be that people use both chains (similar to Bitcoin and Bitcoin Cash), one being more dominant than the other. The main point is whether it be Ethereum 2.0 or Pulse Chain, things are happening to reduce the cost of doing business with the Hex contract.

Proof of Stake Security Model

One of the enormous shifts in blockchain technology is how the network is secured. Traditionally proof of work was the only way to make a currency resistant to a 51% attack. To attack a proof of work secured network would take computational power higher than even a government has. It is an effective way of securing a blockchain. It used to be the only way to secure a blockchain, and the harmful effects it has on the price of the token and the environment were just a necessary evil.

I see many more projects moving to proof of stake, which is much greener for the environment and just as secure. This system for securing the network would incentivise projects to reward people who protect the price, not miners who harm the price to pay for electricity and equipment.

But like anything in the crypto world, proof of stake has its detractors. They say that, in theory, proof of stake could lead to more centralisation (the more conspiratorial calling proof of stake a mechanism by which government could take control). Still, in practice, proof of stake has proved over the years that it can be just decentralised as proof of work (and in some cases more so). Proof of work chains can also suffer from centralisation due to mining hardware only being attainable to a small percentage of people.

Like it or not, projects moving to proof of stake is likely to continue, and its lower fees will help the DeFi ecosystem. In turn, they help the average Joe grow their nest egg for an uncertain future. Even something like Dogecoin, an old fork of Bitcoin, is a proof of stake blockchain, one of the reasons it finds favour with Elon Musk.

AFTERWORD

I hope this book has helped you make an informed decision about another product in the exciting world of DeFi. What will be of Hex in 10 years, who can say? So far, things have been working out as planned. The network and community are growing, the price keeps going up, the interest keeps coming, and people are staking for longer (the average stake length is currently over five years long). But the market is an unpredictable beast. The decisions and reasons for those decisions of millions of people are impossible to know. It takes a lot of information (and faith) to take the risk that a one day, one year or 10-year stake will be worth more then than it is today. We have already had ten years to run the experiment in crypto, it's not going anywhere, and even coins that have not had much to them are still around after years. They will even still occasionally pump, and there is no doubt in my mind that Hex will still be here when that 10-year stake matures, but the state of Hex and the world generally is anybody's guess.

For me, Hex is more than just about earning high interest and the price going up. That is very important to me (and everyone else), and I wouldn't be interested if it didn't. But more than that was the transformation in my thinking when I made my first stake with Hex. As I was "testing the water" and it was such a small amount, I decided to stake it for ten years.

Ten years? Am I unable to touch that wealth for ten years? A genuine (and first for me) gesture of delayed gratification. I had never thought of what things would be like ten years in the future. How old would I be? Which direction will my life be going after such a long period?. Once I had made that 10-year commitment, hopefully giving my future self a little present, it was almost like my whole world had changed. I started to take care of my health to sure my future self is still around to get that payout. I realised I was never going to get rich quick in crypto, not without doing something that is gambling. I like most don't have the capital. I realised I would have to work my ass off and get creative for the next ten years as the Lamborghini will have to wait, which has changed how I approach my work, relationships and health. If Hex is the next crypto to blow up, I won't be able to realise it for ten years. The day to day price doesn't matter, so there is no need to be looking at charts all day every day, freeing me up to do things that add value to society (which I hope this book does). See you in ten years.

If you enjoyed this book I would greatly appreciate an honest review on Amazon

REFERENCES

L. O. C. (2021, January 14). *Richard Heart Hex Crypto *READ THIS* — 2021 Price Prediction, Airdrop, How to Claim for Free or Buy, Scam, Cryptocurrency News, FAQ, Stats, Exchange, Pumpamentals, Uniswap, Hex.com, Mooniswap.* Medium. https://theriz.medium.com/bitcoinhex-launch-airdrop-how-to-claim-buy-scam-snapshot-release-date-46e3a921b7d3

Academy, B. (2020, April 2). *Censorship-resistance.* Binance Academy. https://academy.binance.com/en/glossary/censorship-resistance

Ammous, S. (2018). *The Bitcoin Standard: The Decentralized Alternative to Central Banking* (1st ed.). Wiley.

Benzenoid. (2020, November 30). *Shares are forever.* Hexican Blogs. https://hexicans.info/shares/

Borate, N. (2021, January 11). *What is bitcoin halving and will it affect the rate?* Mint. https://www.livemint.com/money/personal-finance/what-is-bitcoin-halving-and-will-it-affect-the-rate-11610295621496.html

CDS | First Fidelity Guarantee. (n.d.). First Fidelity Guara. Retrieved 15 May 2021, from https://www.firstfidelityguarantee.com/cds

Davis, C. (2021, February 19). *Best Stablecoins • Types of Stablecoins •.* Benzinga. https://www.benzinga.com/money/best-stablecoins-and-4-types-of-stablecoins/#:%7E:text=Stablecoins%20backed%20by%20fiat%20currencies,are%20backed%20with%20dollar%20reserv

Harari, Y. N. (2018). *Sapiens: A Brief History of Humankind* (Reprint ed.). Harper Perennial.

Heart, R. (n.d.-a). *HEX.COM*. Hex.Com. Retrieved 8 April 2021, from https://hex.com/faq/

Heart, R. (n.d.-b). *sciVive.net*. Scivive. Retrieved 1 January 2021, from http://scivive.net/

HEX SHARES EXPLAINED. (2021, April 11). [Video]. YouTube. https://www.youtube.com/watch?v=TqvsFwwzFj8

hodldog. (2021, April 11). *HEX SHARES EXPLAINED* [Video]. YouTube. https://www.youtube.com/watch?v=TqvsFwwzFj8

The Ins and Outs of Financial Instruments. (2020, March 29). Investopedia. https://www.investopedia.com/terms/f/financialinstrument.asp

Kagan, J. (2020, March 11). *Comparing Time Deposit or Certificates of Deposit Rates Between Banks*. Investopedia. https://www.investopedia.com/terms/t/timedeposit.asp

Kennedy, T. (2021, March 26). *Grayscale + The First Blockchain Certificate of Deposit: A Perfect Match*. Medium. https://medium.datadriveninvestor.com/

grayscale-the-first-blockchain-certificate-of-deposit-a-perfect-match-97bc99cb09e3

Landry, D. (2014, May 23). *Bitcoins for the Uninitiated: An Introduction*. Fair Observer. https://www.fairobserver.com/region/north_america/bitcoins-uninitiated-introduction/

M. (2020, March 10). *What is a Certificate of Deposit (CD)? | Pay it less*. Payitless.Com. https://blog.payitless.com/what-is-a-certificate-of-deposit-cd/

Maloney, M. (2015). *Guide To Investing in Gold & Silver: Protect Your Financial Future*. WealthCycle Press.

Mansa, J. (2021, April 5). *How Does Bitcoin Mining Work?* Investopedia. https://www.investopedia.com/tech/how-does-bitcoin-mining-work/

Peterson, J. B. (2018). *12 Rules for Life: An Antidote to Chaos* (Later prt. ed.). Random House Canada.

Rasure, E. (2021, March 31). *Soft Fork Definition.* Investopedia. https://www.investopedia.com/terms/s/soft-fork.asp

Richard Heart. (2020, December 9). *Richard Heart on Bitcoin, Ethereum, HEX and blockchain cryptocurrency! Live, click now! Or doom.* [Video]. YouTube. https://www.youtube.com/watch?v=lP8rWWOGonM

Richard Heart. (2021, April 14). *EMERGENCY! $1M BITCOIN UPDATE! ETHEREUM @ $10,000 FORK today! HEX new ATH.* [Video]. YouTube. https://www.youtube.com/watch?v=Y5qfvNJXJEE

Shares [*Hex Wiki*]. (2020, December 12). Hex Wiki. http://hex.wiki/what-are-shares#:%7E:text=What%20are%20Shares%3F, (plus%20interest)%20in%20return.

Stablecoin. (2020, June 30). Investopedia. https://www.investopedia.com/terms/s/stablecoin.asp

What is a Certificate of Deposit (CD)? (2019, December 12). Investopedia. https://www.investopedia.com/terms/c/certificateofdeposit.asp

yikes. (2020a, October 20). *Hex FUD* [*Hex Wiki*]. Hex.Wiki. http://hex.wiki/hex-fud

yikes. (2020b, October 22). *Shares* [*Hex Wiki*]. Http://Hex.Wiki/What-Are-Shares. http://hex.wiki/what-are-shares

Printed in Great Britain
by Amazon